D0118761

Looking at . . . Allosaurus
A Dinosaur from the JURASSIC Period

Weekly Reader®
BOOKS

Published by arrangement with Gareth Stevens, Inc.
Newfield Publications is a federally registered trademark
of Newfield Publications, Inc. Weekly Reader is a federally
registered trademark of Weekly Reader Corporation.

Library of Congress Cataloging-in-Publication Data

Brown, Mike, 1947-
    Looking at-- Allosaurus/written by Mike Brown; illustrated by Tony Gibbons.
        p. cm. -- (The New dinosaur collection)
    Includes index.
    ISBN 0-8368-1082-1
    1. Allosaurus--Juvenile literature. [1. Allosaurus. 2. Dinosaurs.] I. Gibbons, Tony, ill.
II. Title III. Series.
QE862.S3B76 1994
567.9'7--dc20   93-37056

This North American edition first published in 1994 by
Gareth Stevens Publishing
1555 North RiverCenter Drive, Suite 201
Milwaukee, Wisconsin 53212 USA

This U.S. edition © 1994 by Gareth Stevens, Inc. Created with original © 1993 by
Quartz Editorial Services, Premier House, 112 Station Road, Edgware HA8 7AQ U.K.

Consultant: Dr. David Norman, Director of the Sedgwick Museum of Geology,
University of Cambridge, England.

Additional artwork by Clare Heronneau.

All rights reserved. No part of this book may be reproduced, stored in a
retrieval system, or transmitted in any form or by any means, electronic,
mechanical, photocopying, or otherwise, without the prior written
permission of the copyright holder.

Printed in the United States of America

Weekly Reader Books Presents

Looking at . . . Allosaurus

A Dinosaur from the JURASSIC Period

by Mike Brown

Illustrated by Tony Gibbons

THE NEW
DINOSAUR
COLLECTION

Gareth Stevens Publishing
MILWAUKEE

Contents

Introducing Allosaurus

If you could go back in time to 150 million years ago, you might meet many frightening creatures. Among them would be **Allosaurus** (<u>AL-OH-SAW</u>-RUS), a fierce predator that lived in what we now call North America. **Allosaurus** was a huge beast that walked on two legs. It also had enormous jaws for ripping the flesh of other dinosaurs.

Allosaurus usually roamed around in groups. This made it easier to hunt other dinosaurs for food. But sometimes, **Allosaurus** would eat dead animals found lying in its path.

For plant-eaters especially, the arrival of an **Allosaurus** meant big trouble. The herbivores stood little chance of survival against this prehistoric giant.

What kind of jaws and claws did **Allosaurus** have? How did it hunt? And did it live up to its name, meaning "different reptile?" Read on to get a better picture of this astonishing dinosaur from Jurassic times.

Dangerous

Allosaurus was a giant. From the tip of its snout to the end of its tail, it was about as long as three automobiles.

dinosaur

As you can see, it was also very tall. **Allosaurus**'s head was 16 feet (5 meters) above the ground. And it stood on two strong legs that were as thick as a person's body.

It's not hard to imagine what a ferocious creature **Allosaurus** must have been.

Allosaurus's jaws were filled with over 70 large, sharp teeth. Each one looked like a dagger, with tiny notches down each side —

The most dangerous things about **Allosaurus** were its giant jaws and fearsome claws. Its big head and powerful, short neck helped it tear huge chunks of meat from a victim.

just like a steak knife — for cutting through flesh. It also had powerful muscles in its neck and back. These would have given it tremendous strength, making it possible for **Allosaurus** to overcome even the biggest dinosaurs.

Each of the powerful arms had three fingers with claws on the end. **Allosaurus**'s legs had four-toed feet. These also ended in long, vicious claws.

Allosaurus also had an unusual bump above its eyes, as you can see in this picture.

Jurassic giant

Scientists have dug up many **Allosaurus** bones. Most of these discoveries have been made in the state of Utah in the United States. Scientists have then rebuilt whole skeletons.

If its skull had been much heavier, **Allosaurus** might not have been one of the most fearsome hunters of the Jurassic Period.

Allosaurus had all the typical features of a **Carnosaur**, or meat-eater. It had a huge head, small front limbs, strong back legs, and a long tail.

Allosaurus's skull was massive with many holes in it. These spaces made its head lighter in weight so that it could move it around more easily.

Allosaurus's neck was short and curved and designed to allow easy movement. This was important when biting into its prey.

Allosaurus's legs had to be very strong in order to support its body weight. On its feet, the first toe faced backward, while the other three faced forward. Because the foot was spread over a large area, Allosaurus could carry its weight more easily.

Compared to its legs, however, Allosaurus's arms were small. But they were extremely powerful, ending in three terrible, curved claws. Allosaurus used these to grip its prey.

Allosaurus also used its claws to tear the flesh off carrion — the bodies of dead animals. There is a lot of evidence to suggest that Allosaurus acted mainly as a scavenger, feeding off creatures that were already dead.

Allosaurus's body was squat, ending in a long, tapering tail that helped Allosaurus keep its balance. It held its tail off the ground as it moved.

The first part of Allosaurus to be dug up was a piece of tail bone, discovered in 1869 in Colorado in the United States. But it was not until eight years later that other remains belonging to the same animal were found, and it was given the name *Allosaurus*, meaning "strange reptile."

Many dinosaur bones have special marks on them. These are known as "muscle attachment scars."

By studying these marks, scientists can tell how the muscles were attached to each dinosaur bone. Then, when they compare their findings with what is known about today's animals, they can get a good idea of how the dinosaur behaved. This is how we know Allosaurus was such a powerful animal.

Dinosaur graveyards

The first bones of **Allosaurus** were discovered in what is now the United States in the late nineteenth century. The first piece ever found was a broken tail bone. In 1883, a complete skeleton was discovered.

The best graveyard of **Allosaurus** bones is also in the United States in Utah. It was first excavated in 1927 at a place called the Cleveland-Lloyd Dinosaur Quarry. From their first dig there, paleontologists (scientists who study the remains of prehistoric creatures) produced over 800 dinosaur bones.

One of the richest excavations at this quarry took place between 1960 and 1965. The University of Utah organized a series of digs for dinosaurs. Many institutes from around the world lent money or materials.

Many dinosaur skeletons were dug up. Among them were at least 44 **Allosaurus** — both adults and young.

10

Battle of the giants

A pack of **Allosaurus** was on the lookout for a meal. Up ahead, they spied a herd of giant creatures eating ferns and trees beside a river. These were **Barosaurus** (BAR-O-SAW-RUS).

One **Barosaurus**, however, had moved a little away from the herd. The pack decided this was the one to kill.

Barosaurus were among the largest animals on Earth. The **Allosaurus** could not attack all of them.

The **Barosaurus** had not been aware of danger. But suddenly, it stopped eating, lifted its head, and smelled the air. Something was wrong. It turned around and saw the pack of **Allosaurus** racing toward it.

12

The dinosaur snorted with fear and began lumbering away.

The pack of **Allosaurus** ran faster and was soon close to the large dinosaur that was heading toward a forest. A few **Allosaurus** ran around **Barosaurus** to block its path. The giant could go no further. It turned to face its attackers, lashing its tail at the predators.

The **Barosaurus** screamed in pain. But the pack had tasted blood and could not be stopped. Meanwhile, the **Barosaurus** herd by the river began to move speedily away. They had young ones to protect from the dreaded **Allosaurus**.

The **Allosaurus** pack leapt all over the lone **Barosaurus**. Under the pack's weight and attack, the large dinosaur fell to the ground.

It reared up on two legs, making a frightening sight. But this did not stop the pack.

Quick as a flash, two **Allosaurus** leapt onto the **Barosaurus**'s back. Using their vicious, curved claws, they tore at its body.

Within a couple of minutes, it was dead. The pack of **Allosaurus** could now feed as much as they liked on the **Barosaurus**'s huge body. It would provide them with plenty of meat to satisfy their enormous carnivorous appetites.

13

Jaws!

Allosaurus had huge and powerful jaws. These jaws were lined with sharp teeth that curved backward. This made them perfect for tearing flesh from victims. It also meant that **Allosaurus** could hang on tightly to its prey if the unfortunate victim struggled to escape from its firm hold.

First, **Allosaurus** would grab a chunk of meat in its mouth. Then the upper jaw pulled backward to slice the meat with its razor-sharp teeth. Now the jaws moved outward, widening the mouth, so that **Allosaurus** could swallow as much as possible. It was a greedy predator.

Allosaurus never chewed its food but swallowed great chunks of meat. It even swallowed small animals whole.

Scientists believe **Allosaurus**'s gullet could stretch like elastic. This way, **Allosaurus** could swallow large lumps of flesh whole without the risk of choking on its meal.

Just look at its teeth! They were long and curved backward, so **Allosaurus** could hold on to its prey. The teeth also had serrated edges, just like a steak knife, making it easier for **Allosaurus** to bite into its victims.

If a tooth broke off in a fight, a new one would soon grow in its place.

Its head may have seemed very big, but **Allosaurus**'s skull was actually lightweight. There were spaces between the bones of the skull, which made it less heavy. There were also powerful muscles in **Allosaurus**'s neck and back that helped operate its horrifying jaws. And the sight of such a huge tongue must have been terrifying.

Allosaurus could move its head around very easily — all the better for grabbing its prey!

Hungry hunter

Did **Allosaurus** hunt in groups or by itself? This is still a mystery. Most scientists now think it moved around in packs, just like wolves or the hunting dogs of Africa. By working together, several **Allosaurus** could have brought down the biggest dinosaurs, like **Diplodocus** (DIP-<u>LOD</u>-OH-KUS) or **Barosaurus**, that were sometimes more than twice the size of **Allosaurus**.

But **Allosaurus** may have also hunted by itself. It may have hidden near a pool of water, for example, to watch for animals coming to drink. Then, without warning, **Allosaurus** may have attacked its victim.

Sometimes, **Allosaurus** ate the meat of animals that were already dead. This was much easier than catching live prey.

Or it might have driven off a smaller hunter, such as **Ceratosaurus** (SER-A-TOE-SAW-RUS), and taken anything this dinosaur may have already caught.

The feared **Allosaurus** had hideous talons on all four of its limbs. It used these talons to tear at the flesh of a live victim or carcass.

Allosaurus was not as fast as some dinosaurs. Even so, it could move at more than twice the speed of many of the dinosaurs it hunted. This meant that few stood a chance of escape when chased by this monster.

Scientists believe **Allosaurus** was possibly the most common predator of all in Jurassic times. With so many of them looking for food, smaller creatures had to be on alert.

The world of Allosaurus

Allosaurus lived in the last part of the Jurassic Period, which lasted from 208 to 144 million years ago. By this time, the climate was not as hot as it had once been. It was now damp, sticky, and rainy. The forests contained tall conifers and cycads, which looked like stumpy palm trees.

Allosaurus was not the only dinosaur around.

There were many other kinds. One was **Camptosaurus** (CAMP-TOE-SAW-RUS), which **Allosaurus** often attacked for food. **Camptosaurus** was a plant-eater with a horny, toothless beak. But it had plenty of teeth in its cheeks for chewing leaves. It also had strong legs for running.

Stegosaurus (<u>STEG</u>-OH-<u>SAW</u>-RUS) ate plants, too, but was much better protected than **Camptosaurus**. It had hard plates on its body and a spiky tail that could seriously hurt any dinosaur that attacked it.

One of the biggest dinosaurs of Jurassic times was **Diplodocus**, seen in the background here. It was half as long as an airplane and weighed more than a double-decker bus. This huge beast ate plants and traveled around in herds. It had a very long neck and a long, slim tail.

Other creatures shared **Allosaurus**'s world, too. Winged reptiles called pterosaurs flew through the sky. There were also the first birds, which had teeth in their beaks. In the seas, crocodiles with flippers and other early marine animals swam freely.

The Carnosaurs

Allosaurus (1) belonged to a group of large dinosaurs called **Carnosaurs** — a word that means "meat-eating reptiles." These were all frightening creatures.

All walked or ran on two powerful legs that supported their bodies like pillars.

Their arms were small, but their fingers ended in sharp claws. They all had big heads, long tails, and jaws filled with pointed teeth.

Ceratosaurus (2) was smaller than **Allosaurus** but was also different in two other ways. Each hand had four fingers.

Allosaurus's hands had only three. **Ceratosaurus** also had a bony bump, but it was on its snout and shaped a little like the horn of a rhinoceros.

One of the strangest **Carnosaurs** was **Dilophosaurus** (DIE-LOAF-OH-SAW-RUS) **(3)**. It had a bony crest on its head made up of two plates placed side by side. Nobody knows what the crest was for. This dinosaur did not have very strong jaws, so it may have gotten its food by scavenging, not hunting.

4

Megalosaurus, (MEG-A-LOW-SAW-RUS) **(4)** has a name meaning "great reptile." You can easily see why this ferocious **Carnosaur** deserves to be called by this name!

21

Allosaurus data

Allosaurus hunted and killed other animals — not only smaller plant-eaters, but smaller carnivores as well. It was a very powerful dinosaur.

There are also some mysterious and surprising features about the body of this Jurassic monster.

Powerful legs

Allosaurus, like other **Carnosaurs**, had large, powerful legs. These supported the dinosaur's heavy body, allowing it to stand upright. They also gave it strength to run after and leap onto prey.

Curved claws

Allosaurus's most dangerous weapons were its claws. There were three on each hand and four on each foot. The claws were curved and long and could rip out the insides of another animal in seconds. They also helped **Allosaurus** to cling to, or pin down, its victims.

Certain death faced almost any creature that came face-to-face with **Allosaurus**.

Long skull

The skull of a fully-grown **Allosaurus** was about as long as your entire body. What a big head! You might think it was bound to be very heavy, but it was not. The skull was thin and had large spaces in it — scientists call them "windows" — that helped to reduce the weight. In spite of its enormous body size, **Allosaurus** had a brain that was no larger than that of a kitten! So it is unlikely to have been highly intelligent. Some **Allosaurus** skulls that have been found are much smaller than others, and so they probably belonged to the young.

Weird bump

Above each of **Allosaurus**'s eyes was an unusual, bony bump. No one knows for certain why this was there. But because the bumps were hollow, some scientists think they may have held a salt gland. A gland of this kind helps to rid the body of excess salt. Others suggest that the bump may have been there to make it easier for **Allosaurus** to recognize one another, since many **Carnosaurs** looked alike. This would have been useful at mating time.

GLOSSARY

carcass — the dead body of an animal.

carnivores — meat-eating animals.

conifers — woody shrubs or trees that bear their seeds in cones.

cycads — tropical shrubs or trees that look like thick-stemmed palms.

dig — (noun) a place where scientists make holes in the earth in order to find the remains of ancient animals or civilizations.

excavate — to make a hole by digging.

herbivores — plant-eating animals.

herd — a group of animals that travels together.

pack — a group of similar or related animals.

predators — animals that kill other animals for food.

prey — animals that are killed for food by other animals.

snout — protruding nose and jaws of an animal.

INDEX